on leaves
and flowers
and trees

MONOGRAPH
PUBLISHING

Copyright ©2012 Ralph Wright, OSB

All rights reserved. No part of this book may be reproduced or transmitted in any form or by any means, electronic or mechanical, including photocopying, recording, or by any information storage and retrieval system without permission in writing from the publisher.

Library of Congress Cataloguing-in-Publication data

Wright, Ralph OSB
on leaves and flowers and trees

Design by Ellie Jones
Cover Design by William E. Mathis and Elie Jones
Cover Photo by William E. Mathis
MathisJones Communications, LLC

Published by Monograph Publishing, LLC
1 Putt Lane
Eureka, Missouri 63025
636-938-1100

ISBN# 978-0-9850542-4-3

on leaves
and flowers
and trees

Ralph Wright, OSB

PROLOGUE

"It is the honourable characteristic of Poetry that its materials are to be found in every subject which can interest the human mind" - so read the opening lines of the 'Advertisement' or Prologue to the Lyrical Ballads of Coleridge and Wordsworth published in 1798. After describing the poems that the book contains as 'experimental' Wordsworth, writing anonymously, goes on to say: "It is desirable that readers should not suffer the solitary word 'Poetry,' a word of very disputed meaning, to stand in the way of their gratification; but that while they are perusing this book, they should ask themselves if it contains a natural delineation of human passions, human characters, and human incidents; and if the answer be favorable to the author's wishes, that they should consent to be pleased in spite of that most dreadful enemy of our pleasures, our own pre-established codes of decision."

These poems, too, are offered for the pleasure of the reader whoever he or she may be. They are the product of the past fifteen or twenty years of my life as a monk. It is considered more hazardous these days to put one's 'vision' into poetry: people immediately feel uneasy and talk of propaganda. But perhaps it is when we cease to try to share our deepest thoughts, feelings and beliefs – about God and love and sin and silence and violence and hatred and union and distance and time and eternity – that our poetry ceases to please or to inspire. I would like my poetry to be read and loved not only by poets but also by the non-poet clientele of our world. Men and women of every walk of life and every interest. From those who program computers or punch cash registers to those vice-presidents who make multi-million dollar deals and survey the world through the dark one-way windows of tall buildings. For we all have to cope on an almost daily basis with belief, unbelief, love, loyalty, betrayal, union, violence, pain, ecstasy, joy, depression, sickness, anger and death.

The poems that follow are attempts to capture moments from these common experiences and to hold them up boldly and without shame for others to share. The Christian sees the dark side – sin, tragedy, separation, death. But he also sees the awesome beauty of all that God creates and the extraordinary dignity of Man re-created in Christ and called to share eternally in the intimate life of God. He already experiences in part the peace of his risen Lord and he believes that it is possible here and now to know, in some measure, the deep joy of union with God. He wants his faith to be reflected in his life and in his words for his deepest call is to give to others from his store – of life, of hope, of vision – whatever has been entrusted to him. If these poems are instances of this, I hope they may succeed in communicating a little of this vision especially to those who, perhaps seeing almost nothing hopeful, may be on the verge of opting for despair.

CONTENTS

Prologue	iv
A Wave	2
A Young Willow Fountain of Ice	3
Above my Bed	4
African Violet	5
As Light Withdraws	6
August	7
Barley	8
Butterfly	9
Caterpillar	10
Childhood	11
Crocuses	12
Day-Lilies in October	13
Elegance	14
The Eve of Falling	15
Everything Is in Reflection	16
Fall Beauty	17
Fall Mood	18
Fall	19
Flightlight	20
Frostscape	21
Glass Branches	23
His Moods	24
I Know a Man Who Has a Feel for Leaves	25
I Like the Still Days	26
I Listened to the Sound of Rain	27
I Will Write of Moments	28
If Death	29
Leaf Fall	30
Leaf Letters	31
Leaf Shadows	32
Leafscape	33
Leaves of Water	34
Leaves	35

Let the Clouds Rain down the Just One	36
Light upon a Lavender Leaf	37
Limelight	38
Mist too Can Be Memorable	39
Orchid	41
Parting	42
Redwoods Soar	43
Reflections	45
Rose	46
Rosepetal	47
The Shadow of the Wind	48
Stillness	49
St. Louis Freezing Rain	50
In Memory of George	51
The Story of Time	52
The Tree	53
Theophany	54
Truncate	55
Two Trees	56
The Valley Trees	57
Windchimer at Dawn	59
God spoke	60
Willow Shadows	61
Fr. Ralph Wright Biography	62
Other Books by Fr. Ralph	63

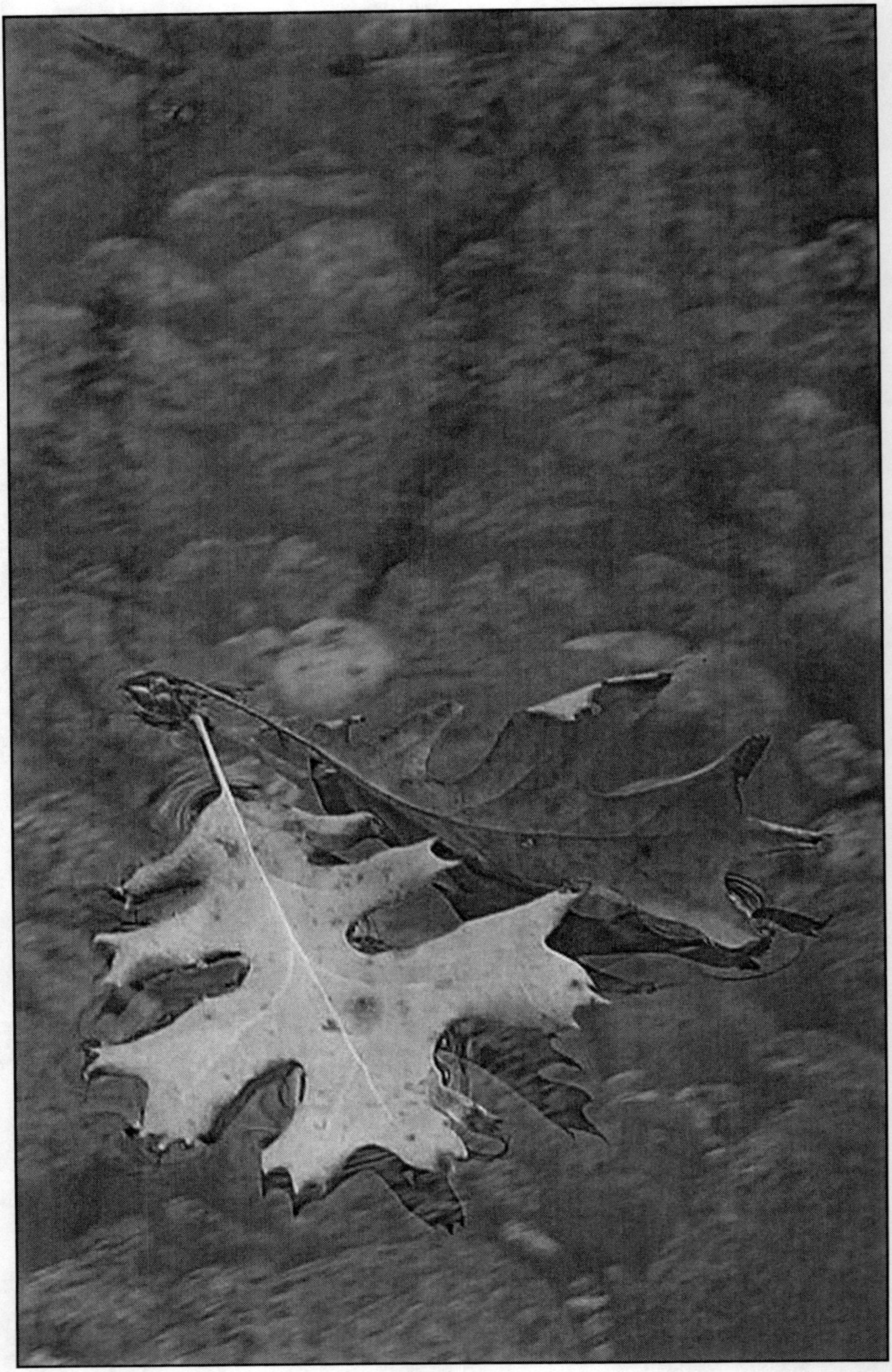

on leaves
and flowers
and trees

A WAVE

a wave
of thanksgiving
like tear gas
hits me:

God hides
so completely
so discreetly

my senses
geigercount
his glory
in the rose

faith reaches
beyond

where all the light
of all the galaxies
is but a candle

so discreetly
so completely

thank you

A YOUNG WILLOW FOUNTAIN OF ICE

a young willow fountain of ice
this morning after Matins
against a rose January sky —
a masterpiece of curves in crystal
of haunting mauve beauty

blending the essentially gentle
giving receiving circle of compassion
with the straight brittle seize and take
battle line of ultimata —
the Yes or No intransigence
of arrogance

an angry impatience
at the evil
in every heart even our own
that leaves a litany
of booted limbs
protruding from
Napoleonic snow

ABOVE MY BED

above my bed
hang three paintings
of mountain flowers
in yellow and red
with dark green leaves

reflected
in the glass
that frames them
are the trees
outside the window
dark branches
untouched by dawn light

way back
behind the trees
the sky is blue
behind the mountains

and the sun
crawls
down the mountainside
devouring like lava
the remnants of the night

AFRICAN VIOLET

kept by every kind of shade
from seeing
face to face
your golden Maker,
dreaming of being
back in the permanent gloom
of Jungle Giants,
you peer from regal purple
like the moon at midnight
and reach
— on tiptoe —
out for the kiss of sunlight

AS LIGHT WITHDRAWS

Over the snow
ripples of gold
touched with amber
flow into long
blue-grey shadows
a few sparrows
peck scattered sunflower seeds
against the night

oak leaves dead from November
but still hanging
tighten trembling fists or poise
in total stillness
the cold grows and grows
as light withdraws
silence gradually falls

AUGUST

the first small leaves
of maple trees
are falling
through the shade
towards the yet
uncovered ground
and as they fall
I see them for
they twice hit sunlight

BARLEY

I have not seen a barley field so still
under the cover of a wide grey sky
as here at 6.00 a.m. in mid July
deep in the farming countryside
near Nether Wallop

the silence of the fields
is reinsured
by the soundproofing of the narrow lanes
made Romanesque or Norman
by their arching trees and tall hedges
with here and there a stretch of pure tunnel
into the light and wonder of a sky
stretching above the barley

there is a kind of silence here
that I have not seen
since the February silence
of a morning frost
that patterned pine trees on the inside
of my bedroom window
near Mt Vernon, Illinois
at 5.00 a.m. way back in '82.

BUTTERFLY

am I just a
pub-crawling butterfly
pollen-sozzled in the dazzle world
of infinite transient flowerdom
flitting in poiseworthy
playful mastery
with eyes for wings
sometimes glad of sunlight
swooping with crescendo silence
nectaring my days away
and leaving in my wake
a litany of colors
unconcerned for time
blending a blinding
eye-transcendent wing-speed
with careless summer doziness
about direction
who can dream me a
being more all round
infinite in beauty
than this drunk with joy
utterance of God
reveling in its finite
casual glory
caught by sunlight fluttering
on the storm's brink
almost conscious that each moment
is eternal
and seeming to be almost proud
of being no more tomorrow

CATERPILLAR

thoughts on weeding

the caterpillar
   chews and chews
deliberately
   on greens and blues

does he with joy
   accept his fate
a munching, crawling,
   stalk-bound state

or does he in
   the dark of night
dream of the ecstasy
   of flight

till from his tomb
   like Egypt's kings
he soars on silent
   cosmic wings

and nectar unconceived
   before
sips from a brief
   ambrosial straw?

CHILDHOOD

Why can't eternity start at ten
or nine and a half in the sunlight
with vigor and life and laughter
and surgings of joy
and bubblings of almost-still-innocence
why can't eternity start
let time stop
who wants to be
older
or wiser
or more disillusioned
but fools
come Lord stop the clock
break into with music
our premature longing
amber the
caught-in-a-moment-of-cobweb-sunshine
fly of our childhood
and keep us
in laughter and song
excitement and mystery
playfully searching and dancing
through woods of discovery
through all eternity too
wonderfully poised
towards you

CROCUSES

the crocuses pregnate the sky
at dawn in violet white and gold
I wonder why
but am not told
 —perhaps I am too old—
the crocuses are big with dew
at dawn in yellow white and blue
I wonder why
but am not told
I wonder who
but am too old

DAY-LILIES IN OCTOBER

Who'd have thought that day-lilies would bloom
in this Fall frost
heavy at the end of October

yet two lilies towered
above their fallen comrades
— one budded and one bloomed.

I thought of a speaker system left standing
as the tents were struck
and the traveling circus prepared to move on.

Behind the lilies leaves were drifting down
methodically like marines
yellow and gold and amber in the sun

that hit them broadside
from behind the trees
as they fell into its glare.

Michael said quietly that all the seasons
— Spring, Summer, Fall, Winter —
were suddenly here.

While John, who planted the lilies,
had gone like the leaves
to where

beyond the thorn of roses he may trumpet radiance
in the new Eden
of God's undarkened day..

ELEGANCE

all our Empire States
our Eiffel Towers
our Leaning Towers of Pisa
falter before
the elegance of grass

a few tall strands of which
outlined against the trailer
move in the morning light

even the freshly sculpted
concrete lamp posts at the 270/64 crossover
reaching towards the sky
with such apparent competence
fail before its nonchalance

and when we all have gone
and our buildings have crumbled
it will still sway
eloquently
above the sand

THE EVE OF FALLING

like leaves more glorious on the eve of falling
caught radiant in October light
or swallows flexing for the long migration
valued now for their impending flight
so now your face your eyes your laughter
I watch with a wonder touched with sorrow
knowing that my God in you
— this blaze — will not be here tomorrow

EVERYTHING IS IN REFLECTION

everything is
in reflection

the planets
pieces of dead star
by night
are big with sunlight

the trees
on the tip of the canyon
still black with night
are white with sunlight

the dark pools
at the bend of the North Platte
echoing the crags above
are bronze
with sunlight

and you
in this huge darkness
in this ten millionth part of time
and this ten billionth part of space
look at me
with what I think is godlight

FALL BEAUTY

reflected in the window of the door
aslant against the midnight purple wall
the leaves outside are dancing in the wind
in yellow amber green and sudden gold

so great an exhibition of His work
in casual excess
is always hard to find
and yet

the claim is limited
that one brief leaf may have on our concern
while God
to whom you'd think we would appear as leaves
has proved the hold we have upon his heart
unlimited

FALL MOOD

Trees get more beautiful
as I get older
more stately as they drop their leaves
in sunlight or in shade.

The clouds control the sunbeams,
storing or releasing them
with casual precision,
to wend their way down
among the branches
kindling as they go.

As though some great conductor
nonchalant in mastery,
with one finger,
was bringing in the flutes
to join the symphony
but then
before we might enjoy their fiery dance
moving the clouds over,
to check the probing sunlight,
till all the heat of color now is gone
and dusk comes down like winter
on the scene.

FALL

there is a breeze today and yet
no leaves are falling

yesterday was still but leaves were drifting
slowly through sunlight into shade

who knows the moment of detachment
lift-off into nothingness or touch-down into loam

is someone somewhere calling
even the leaves by name?

FLASHLIGHT

a white window of sky
—two feet by ten—
at the top of the wall of windows
that show just buildings

a stark tree
with only a few
December leaves
left on the branches

eight Canadian geese
soar diagonally
across the grey-white canvas
up, up,
and are gone

FROSTCAPE

a poised still
world of intensive
beauty and silence
branches clothed with
icicle swords
marshaled on minute twigs and planned
to pin-point perfection
caught in the sudden
electronic flash of the
midnight frost that
struck in a moment of melting
O how the
night of my
almost Tchaikovsky
Sleeping Beauty of magic
O how the time stood
still while I did not
dare to breathe as the
breath of death
passed white
leaving stunned and delicate
dancing fairy arithmetic
caught like a
crystal humming-bird
silkworm finery
regal omnipotent
moment of proud
atomic material glory
O for me poise
poise poise
in infinite silence
live in your motionless
time-unravished virginity

be for me pristine and eternal
be for me captured and still
but be living still

GLASS BRANCHES

Ice stormed and crackled through the night
leaving at dawn glass branches
dipped in rose to diamond as the sun
emerged to scan the final freeze.

Too blinding beautiful this wake
— but devious too .
The broken limbs beneath the crushing ice
cast spells of wonder on our fickle hearts.
How blinding when her charms so lightly make
even death beautiful.

HIS MOODS

He knows what deep means—
grief sometimes
hangs upon his features—
sometimes he is beckoned by despair
and is happy
only with no one—
his flights of pleasure
are like dark trees
poplars against a blue sky
ruffled by wind—
and somewhere in between is peace—
the presence of evening with a dying sun
people returning
rooks calling
into the distance—
peace is the silence which he does not hear
the smile or quiet laughter of contentment
breaking gently
almost undetected
into being

I KNOW A MAN WHO HAS A FEEL FOR LEAVES

I know a man who has a feel for leaves
and treats them kindly as one might a friend
he feels that if a human being was cloned
and multiplied like paperbacks or waves
they still would have a being of their own
and would when gone be left in separate graves

so why not have a reverence for each leaf
like this one from an oak tree on this path
reaching like a hand towards who knows
what dying ecstasy as the slow breeze
helps it find a resting place or home
in the recycling earth?

He feels that it is worth
a moment's silence and believes
that anyone who ever has seen war
or heard of famines, floods or on the news
has watched the havoc that an earthquake strewed
with men and mountains in its wake ignored
— or even watched a stadiumfull applaud —
will pause with wonder as he looks and breathes
and also have a little time for leaves.

I LIKE STILL DAYS

I like the still days
in autumn
when the wind has died

and leaves drop
one by one
simply because they have to

their clinging power
of yesterday is gone
and in the sunlight
they go all the way

like late arrivals
singly
down to join
the concert-goers in the foyer

waiting for the buzzer
to call them
to take their seats
for the silent symphony
of winter
to begin

I LISTENED TO THE SOUND OF RAIN

I listened to the sound of rain
upon the leaves
approaching with the wind
— the rain and wind were still some woods away

I listened to the terror of the wind
upon the leaves in anger tearing them
untimely out of life and swirling them
at random in the dark upon the ground

I listened to the calm that came
from nowhere on the leaves
when suddenly the angry air was gone
I heard them welcome with relief
the newborn silence of the night
and watch in awe for dawn

I WILL WRITE OF MOMENTS

I will write of moments
tasted together — new wine —
to a background of confident
rhythmical stark 'griechische Musik'
untouched by dreams.
I will write in thanks
for the simple joy
of finding a friend
whom — if I were God —
I would have created.
I will write of what must remain
forever wordless
— thoughts
caught in the frail
net of the intellect —
for only the heart
really can tell
(but cannot being tongueless)
of what I am writing —
and writing now
before the snow falls
and the slow song of autumn
dies in the distance
and before this moment
is lost in the sunlight
the misted sunlight
of smouldering leaves —
and now I have said
almost nothing
and it is written.

IF DEATH

if death
is not
the doorway to life
then I
am just
a superior leaf
hanging a season
out of the sky
then falling briefly
into the earth
small manure
barely enough
to properly dung a rose with.

LEAF FALL

I was not watching but I heard
a leaf fall off an indoor plant just now
and hit the carpet in the perfect stillness —
as it fell it touched another leaf
and so I heard its fall —
there was no kind of wind or other force
to cause this brief event, it seems it fell
simply because it had been growing
silently old long enough
to earn this parting —
it may be at least a week or even a month
before another leaf from the same plant
merits this moment
so what a simple grace and gift it was,
and quite uncalled for,
to be there at this instant not to watch
— as one might watch a lift-off towards the moon —
but, as befits its call to be discreet,
only to hear the falling of this leaf.

LEAF LETTERS

you sent me letters in the leaves today
written with various colors
each one a unique blend
of rain and sun and drought and cold

I had not noticed till I saw in one
— a single maple leaf —
the red the green the yellow and the brown
and recognized your hand

I caught them with the camera
in case the colors should have changed tomorrow
now I know they were addressed to me
and through me to your people

LEAF SHADOWS

the movement of
the light upon the
floor mimics

the movement of
the branches of
the willow without leaves

if there is no
color
in your movement
where is your music?

LEAFSCAPE

there is a silence in the patience of the leaves
waiting in stillness for the breath of Fall
all the silence of the desert wastes
when no one roamed the planet —
there is a waiting in their watching mood
a resignation to a job well done
they clung to branches yesterday as wind
wrestled with them to release their hold
then drifted to a gentler breeze today
that rippled on the amber and the gold
with all the sigh of loam

LEAVES OF WATER

I wonder did
   God think of leaves
      falling from
         the autumn trees

before he thought
   of flakes of snow
      leaves of water
         drifting so

gently in
   December's breeze
      they might have been
         October's leaves

LEAVES

leaves
have become
— like Monet's lilypads —
part of my paradise

LET THE CLOUDS RAIN DOWN THE JUST ONE

like a child
blowing bubbles
out of liquid glass
tips of needles
from a silver fir
bud dewdrop crystals
in the drizzle mist
this grey December day
preparing
— if the cloud should lift —
waterford micro-galaxies of light
to spellbind instant glory

LIGHT UPON A LAVENDER LEAF

Light upon a lavender leaf in Fall
seen from beneath
perhaps the greatest mystery of all
in stark relief—
the happy blend of circular and straight,
poise and motion,
in simple sunlight, dignity in shape,
against an ocean
of background shadow hoping to be given
at least tomorrow
in which to find, without being rudely driven
by pain or sorrow,
an apt moment good enough for parting,
easy to accept,
a way of greeting other loam in darkness
without regret.

LIMELIGHT

The angle of the sun
between the trees
hits this blade of grass
arching it against a background
of darkened shaded green

the unique solar
angle of the year
between the trees
metes out
only thirty seconds
of nonchalant
parabolic
total glory
then returns the blade
without ceremony
to ordinary darkness

all the silence
and reserve
of a Japanese print

a single exclamation point
to start the day

MIST TOO CAN BE MEMORABLE

Mist too can be memorable
drifting at daybreak or at noon
over quiet water
or under the eave of reaching oaks
that tower above and stretch imperious
above the seaweed while the leaves waver
and the waves wait

tides remain our timepiece
steadily changing with their ebb and flow
— the tragicomedy
of human history —
heaving up or swallowing
the debris of the years

we wait
for ecstasy or suffering
to pass —
we watch
winter stillness break to movement
dance a while in warmth upon a branch
and fall golden
into the shadows

we hear
gulls that sing and squabble for their food
without thanksgiving
(moaning across the water or poised on garbage)
to an unknown God —

we know
moods that knive us raw apart
words that scalpel

and moments of oneness
too deep for sound
suffered in silence

we have watched and listened
and have heard
beyond the mist that drifts
over the quiet water
the wind swaying in the leaves above the sea
that it is good to be

ORCHID

The Parthenon, the Taj Mahal, Saint Peter's Rome
-— Man's finest hour —
all stammer and are mute before
the architecture of a flower.

PARTING

Distance leaves a
wake of autumn
forests waiting
for curling smoke
down through deep
white tombs of winter
until the urgency
of spring
bursts sudden green
cascading down
in gentle laughter
towards fulfillment

REDWOODS SOAR

Redwoods soar
into their own silence
creating a calm richer
than the calm of graveyards
or of ruined abbeys
or even of pyramids —
their silence in the sunlight
is more intense
and their shadow
teaches the full mystery of light
conveying
the majesty of seasons and of change —
their utter stillness
makes a way
for measured movement —
in their light and darkness are displayed
endless patterns of beauty
at their feet and in their shade
grass waves carefully
throwing a casual shadow —
even insects find
in their silence and against
their darkness
their own bright place for being
poised or darting
like a scratch across a window pane
fast to another poise —
here
silence is sacred
I feel a need
to ask permission to breathe
speech seems almost sacrilegious
even thought seems out of place

and I am at ease
only with wonder —
shade from the tall
sundial trees
tells it is already
after noon and soon
only the tops of the tallest trees
will be able to tell
— for a little while longer —
the glory of sunlight

REFLECTIONS

The prism of the mind explodes the world
into a million colors
a dazzling university
with too little time for wonder

wonder at the way a leaf may fall
simply at evening into half-still waters
that till this moment held a silent face
peering
out at the dying day.

ROSE

from folded bud
to open bloom
you move like royalty
knowing yourself adored

accepting from
the silence of the dawn
your sole applause
you move
from youth towards magnificence
while the proud mates
of potentates
for dignity
borrow your fragrance

your colors are
the arbiters of excellence
all bow
before your being

when the symphony is over
and you die
Eden is empty

ROSEPETAL

a single petal
of a rose
brown and dry
with age
marked the place
I had reached
in a book
unopened
for twenty years

the glamour
of the living dawn
was gone

but in its place
in various shades
of coffee, fawn and brown
— from where the petals once had held the stem —
a great tree
spread its tendrils
like a fan
revealing
in the harmony
of its quiet symmetry
a hint of some great beauty
yet to come
still somehow ambered in the Maker's mind

I barely noticed that the blood was gone

THE SHADOW OF THE WIND

I have seen with you
the shadow of the wind
thrown by tall trees
guarding the dark water
the shadow of the wind
keeping a certain calm
against the constant turbulence
of changing light and darkness
I have seen in you and known
the shadow of the wind
as clouds race white and black
across the sky
and in this calm I found
a joy that cannot fear
what dark may do to me beyond
the shadow of the wind.

STILLNESS

stillness
this morning
is charged
with meaning
every tree
every leaf
every twig
perfectly at rest
till a squirrel
in stop-go motion
interjects
a flash of
movement
then disappears
and all the
landscape
however hurtling
thru unending space
is caught again
poised
in unbreathing
stillness
waiting
for the cameraman
under the beige blanket
to close the shutter

ST. LOUIS – FREEZING RAIN, POSTLUDE

The icicles are trees this morning
in crystal wonderlands that burst the heart
all the Fabergés of every art
since cave men sketched their bison on the walls
are children building castles on the sand
compared to these —
twigs and limbs with every hang of ice
poise paradise in filaments of light
splintered through a million perfect prisms
throwing a circuit-breaker in our heads
lest overload should burn away the mind
and leave us foolish

and yet You chose in wisdom to forego
this icescape ecstasy when You came
to live a lifetime here so long ago
if You had come to Palestine today
You could yourself have seen with your own eyes
this sparkle kingdom that was gone by noon
with your own eyes You could yourself have seen
and then been
back at the Beautiful Gate for evening prayer
by special Concorde via Tel Aviv
to hear the bombs go off and drink the wine
and see the sun go down and yet You chose
to see it all through mine.

IN MEMORY OF GEORGE

the leaves are wild today
excited and exciting in the breeze
October sunlight breaks the palette wide
and gold and amber, yellow brown and green
run crazy in their blaze against the sky
the sky too is recharged with greys and blues
and cumulus and storm clouds ride the wind

it speaks of your impatience to be free
free to utter galaxies with God
(or bring another Still Life into being)
Simone Weil once wrote that the Almighty
chose abdication when he thought up Time
she said God thought up Time and like a beggar
upon the busy sidewalk of the city
waits silently for the crumbs of love
which in good time we throw him
and Art, she said, lies in the waiting.

THE STORY OF TIME

the story of time is told in every leaf
the blending mooded spectrum of them all
needing the drumming open stage of time
to conjugate the splendor of their being

those like us with mind might need only
instants to say 'Yes' and to be whole
like spirits on a needlehead of 'No'
but leaves require the pageantry of Fall
to dance their glory down into the grime

THE TREE

the tree
exploded out of
winter silence
throwing shooting
stars of blossom
into the lake
where the sun
burnt
the evening away
and left no ashes

THEOPHANY

A fine dry
stalk structure
on which are poised
with total symmetry
tiny wind-blown
toy umbrellas
forming a perfect
Fabergé sphere —
a Czar's jewel
beyond fury
good for nothing
but reflecting glory —
Yellow Goatsbeard
a dead weed
ripe
for launching seed.

TRUNCATE

Redwood trees
have soared in silence
for thousands of years
along our shores
their age
their calm
their dignity
command respect

scions thrusting
from the roots of Jesse
across our land
towards eternity
are axed daily
without awe
out of being

TWO TREES

two trees
proclaim in spring
a word to the world

one exploding
into blossom
trumpets glory

one stretching
dead limbs
holds the empty
body of God

both speak
with due reserve
into the listening
ear of the world

THE VALLEY TREES

even the cars and vans that sweep
smoothly up the twisting ribbon of road
cannot intrude upon the peace
rolled out before my eyes

the western light slants low across the valley
throwing long shadows — all of my life
so easily might have been so nearly was
declined or conjugated here in nouns and verbs
like running, marching, catching, kicking, coaching,
the Gym, the Bounds, the Rugger Fields, the Courts
and all the different light that hits these trees

the winter evenings stark with the lovely truths
of bare branches, skeletons letting through
the various greens before the sudden dark

the winter mornings with the ground frost
spread out like silk upon the valley floor
and tinged blood purple by the frail sun

the summer mornings with the distant trees
rising like islands from a haunting mist
and lazy summer evenings with the occasional crack
of bat on ball and a few hands
offering their casual comment of applause

all this so many worlds away
from what my life in various ways has seen
but which sees now

    — without the sadness of dismembered dreams —
this silent beauty — knowing myself too

reflected in the light that paints
stillness on these winter trees
hauling the end in, hand over hand,
of another day

WINDCHIMER AT DAWN

Without the wind
you are as silent
as a sundial
on a cloudy day

today

for thirty minutes
you hung unchimed
while I watched
the maple leaf
outlined
against the
O so brief
morning mist
in total stillness
unchime
the day

GOD SPOKE

God
spoke
to Elijah
in a gentle breeze
but after a storm
leaves
at sundown
in total stillness
have their own eloquence

WILLOW SHADOWS

thrashing willow branches
—switches in the breeze
against the sun —
throw every kind of shadow
on the ground
writhing at my feet

some soft
some stark
some bright
some dark

they nonchalantly blend
in greys and blacks a symphony of light
spontaneously revealing
marvels in the mystery of their movement

improvising in this silent dance
they capture all the transience of time
projecting
on the screen that is the mind
the casual disorder of their being

BIOGRAPHY OF RALPH WRIGHT, O.S.B.

Ralph Wright was born in Nottinghamshire, England, about 200 yards from Sherwood Forest on October 13, 1938. He was christened David Grant Melville Wright. His father, Monty Wright, was a mining engineer responsible for the coal mines of the Butterley Company. Five generations of the family had been involved in this Derbyshire company since it's foundation in 1790. David went to High School at Ampleforth College whence he won a minor scholarship in Classics to Pembroke College, Oxford. Deciding to spend two years doing his National Service before going to Oxford, he joined the Sherwood Foresters, was commissioned and spent a year in Malaya as a platoon commander, partly in the jungle, partly at the base camps. In 1969, on emerging from the army, he joined the Benedictine Community at Ampleforth Abbey in Yorkshire taking the name Ralph (pronounced Rafe) after the Derbyshire martyr, Ralph Sherwin.

Having completed his BA in Greats (Classics, Ancient History & Philosophy) at Oxford and his STL in Theology at Fribourg (Switzerland) he was ordained priest at Ampleforth Abbey on July 5, 1970. A month later, he left England, at the Abbot's invitation, to join the St. Louis Priory – the community's foundation in the United States. When the monastery became independent in July, 1973, he opted to become a permanent member of the newly independent house. Shortly thereafter, he became an American citizen. Fr. Ralph initially taught Latin, Greek, English and Religion in the St. Louis Priory School. In 1978, he was made Novice Master. He has been the Varsity Tennis coach on and off for over 25 years and Vocation Director for the community for about 20. Currently, besides running the Varsity tennis program and coordinating community efforts to attract vocations, he teaches Theology to the 11th grade, Creative Writing to seniors, and is Advisor in the School.

OTHER BOOKS BY FR. RALPH WRIGHT

Wild...
They Also Serve: Tennis, a Global Religion
Leaves of Water
Seamless
Life is Simpler Toward Evening
Ripples of Stillness
Perhaps God
Christ Our Love for All Seasons
Our Daily Bread
The Eloquence of Truth
Mostly Vertical Thoughts

Over 50 Hymns